BUG BOOKS

Daddy Longlegs

Catherine Anderson

Heinemann Library
Chicago, IL

Customer Service 888-454-2279
Visit our website at www.heinemannlibrary.com

Design: Kimberly R. Miracle and Cavedweller Studio
Illustration: Will Hobbs

Color Reproduction by Dot Gradations Ltd, UK
Printed and bound in China by South China Printing Company

12 11 10 09 08
10 9 8 7 6 5 4 3 2 1

New edition ISBNs: 978 1 4329 1237 6 (hardcover)
                      978 1 4329 1248 2 (paperback)

The Library of Congress has cataloged the first edition as follows:
    Anderson, Catherine, 1974-
      Daddylonglegs / Catherine Anderson.
        p. cm. — (Bug books)
    Summary: Describes the physical characteristics, habits, and natural environment of the tall spiderlike daddylonglegs.
    Includes bibliographical references (p.   ).
     ISBN: 1-40340-763-0 (HC), 1-40340-994-3 (Pbk.)
     1. Opiliones- - Juvenile literature. [1. Daddy longlegs.] I. Title. II. Series.
    QL458.5 .A53 2003
    595.4'3- -dc21

                 2002004361

Acknowledgments
The publishers would like to thank the following for permission to reproduce photographs:
© Ann & Rob Simpson p. 21; © Bryan E. Reynolds p. 25; © Corbis pp. 17 (Michael & Patricia Fogden), 23 (Michael T. Sedam); © FLPA (Jeremy Early) p. 18; © Getty Images (Photodisc) p. 20; © James C. Cokendolpher pp. 7 (left), 9, 26; © James H. Robinson p. 7 (right); © James P. Rowan p. 5; © JLM Visuals (Richard P. Jacobs) p. 16; © John S. Reid p. 10; © NHPA (Haroldo Palo Jr.) p. 22; © Oxford Scientific Films pp. 6 (David Fox), 11 (Marshall Black); © Photo Researchers Inc. pp. 15 (Stephen Dalton), 28 (Stephen P. Parker), 29 (Gary Retherford); © Scott Braut pp. 19, 24; © Stuart Wilson p. 8; © Visuals Unlimited pp. 4 (Jonathan D. Speer), 12 (Mary Cummins), 13 (Bill Beatty); © William E. Ferguson pp. 14, 27.

Cover photograph of a daddy longlegs walking across a leaf reproduced with permission of Getty Images (National Geographic/Brian G. Green).

The publishers would like to thank Dr. William Shear, Department of Biology, Hampden-Sydney College, for his assistance in the preparation of the first edition of this book.

Contents

What Are Daddy Longlegs? 4

How Big Are Daddy Longlegs?. 8

How Are Daddy Longlegs Born?. 10

How Do Daddy Longlegs Grow? 12

How Do Daddy Longlegs Move?. 14

What Do Daddy Longlegs Eat? 16

Which Animals Attack Daddy Longlegs?. 18

Where Do Daddy Longlegs Live? 20

How Long Do Daddy Longlegs Live? 22

What Do Daddy Longlegs Do? 24

How are Daddy Longlegs Special?. 26

Thinking About Daddy Longlegs 28

Bug Map 30

Glossary. 31

Index 32

More Books to Read 32

Some words are shown in bold, **like this**. You can find out what they mean by looking in the glossary.

What Are Daddy Longlegs?

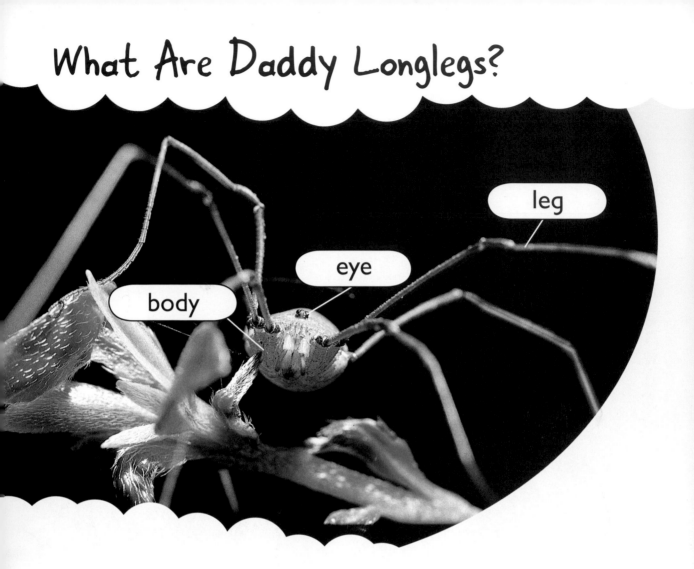

leg

eye

body

A daddy longlegs has a round body and eight very skinny legs. The legs are covered with short hairs. A daddy longlegs has two eyes on the top of its body.

4

Daddy longlegs are **arachnids**.
They are related to **spiders**. But
they are not real spiders. They do
not make **webs**.

Some people call this **spider** a daddy longlegs. But it is a cellar spider. It is a real spider. It spins a **web**.

You can see two body parts on a real spider. A daddy longlegs' body parts are joined together in one piece.

spider

daddy longlegs

How Big Are Daddy Longlegs?

A daddy longlegs can bend its long legs in many places. Some have front legs as long as your hand.

The body of a daddy longlegs is usually the size of your smallest fingernail. But it can be as big as a grape! **Male** daddy longlegs are smaller than **females**.

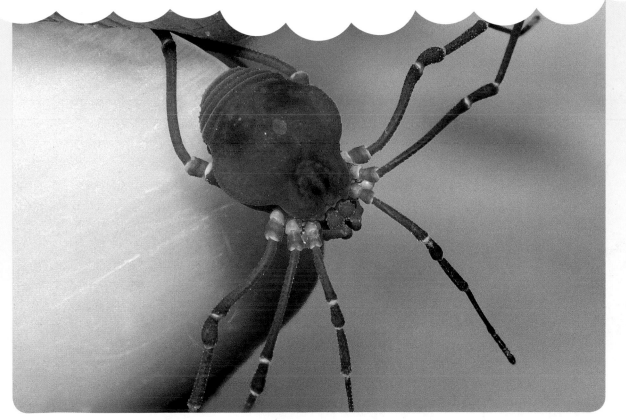

How Are Daddy Longlegs Born?

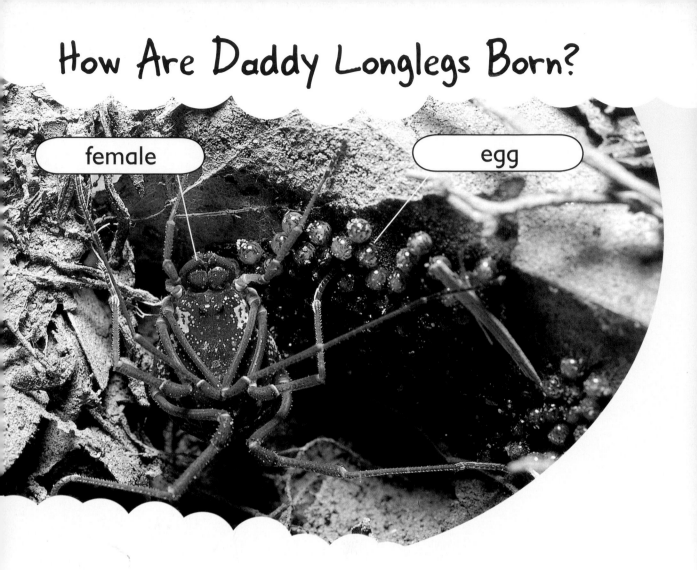

female

egg

Daddy longlegs **mate** in the fall. The **female** lays 20 to 30 tiny eggs. She lays them in wet ground. The eggs stay in the ground through the winter.

The eggs **hatch** in the spring.
Baby daddy longlegs look like their
parents. They are very tiny. Each one
is smaller than the period at the end
of this sentence.

11

How Do Daddy Longlegs Grow?

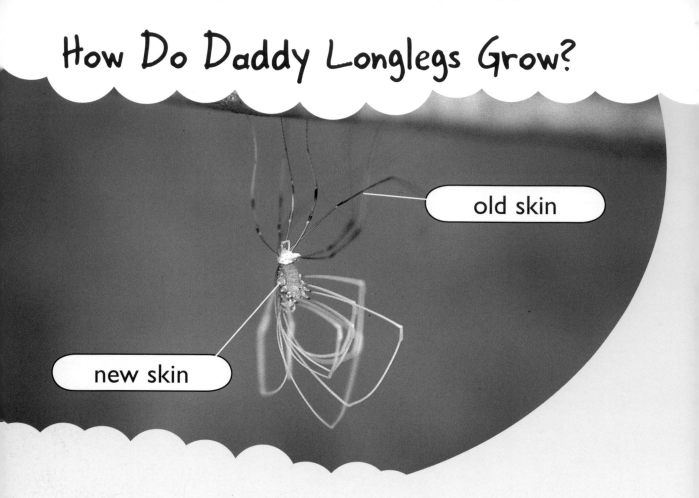

old skin

new skin

As a baby daddy longlegs grows, its skin gets too small. The skin splits down the back. The daddy longlegs slowly crawls out of the old skin. There is a new skin underneath. This is called **molting**.

Young daddy longlegs molt every 10 days. They grow bigger after each molt. After two to three months, they are adults.

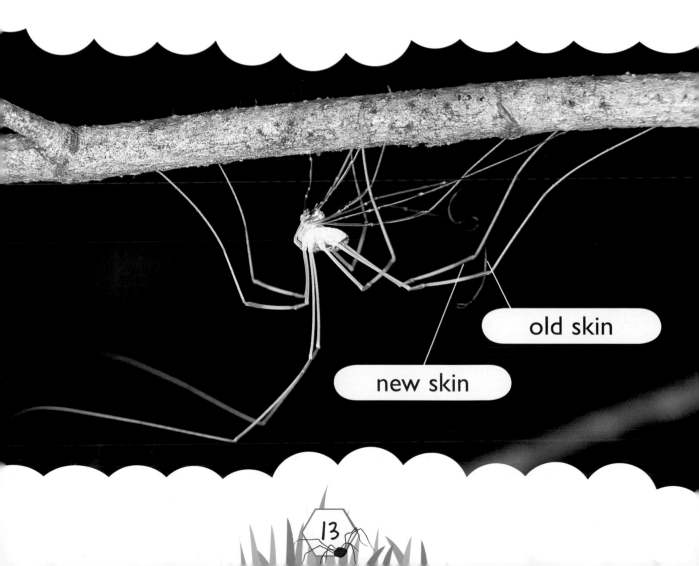

old skin

new skin

How Do Daddy Longlegs Move?

Daddy longlegs move using their eight legs. They can run very fast. They can also climb up walls or trees.

At the end of each leg is a small claw. Daddy longlegs use these claws to hold on to things. They can even hang upside-down.

What Do Daddy Longlegs Eat?

Some daddy longlegs eat fruit and flowers. Others are **predators**. They eat small insects, snails, and worms. Some daddy longlegs are **scavengers**. They eat dead animals.

Daddy longlegs have mouthparts that work like small scissors. They break the food into tiny pieces.

Which Animals Attack Daddy Longlegs?

parasite

Sometimes red **parasites** live on daddy longlegs. They can hurt them. Birds, ants, and **spiders** all eat daddy longlegs.

The legs of a daddy longlegs come off easily. If a **predator** pulls off a leg it will keep wiggling. The predator watches the leg while the daddy longlegs runs away.

Where Do Daddy Longlegs Live?

Daddy longlegs live all over the world. They live under logs and rocks and on tree trunks. Most live in warm, wet places. Some live in the desert.

In some places, daddy longlegs live in a group. They all wiggle when a **predator** is near. This may scare the predator away.

How Long Do Daddy Longlegs Live?

Daddy longlegs live for about one year.
Most types of daddy longlegs die soon
after they **mate**.

Some daddy longlegs are **endangered**.
People go into daddy longlegs' **habitats**
such as this cave. This disturbs them and
they cannot live there anymore.

What Do Daddy Longlegs Do?

Daddy longlegs cannot see well. They use their legs to hear, taste, and smell. Tiny hairs on their legs help them feel things. Daddy longlegs **preen** their legs to keep them clean.

Daddy longlegs do not have **fangs** or **venom**. They cannot hurt other animals by biting. But some daddy longlegs use the spines on their legs to pinch.

spine

How are Daddy Longlegs Special?

If a **predator** pulls a leg off a daddy longlegs, it will still live. A daddy longlegs cannot grow a new leg, but it can live without one or two.

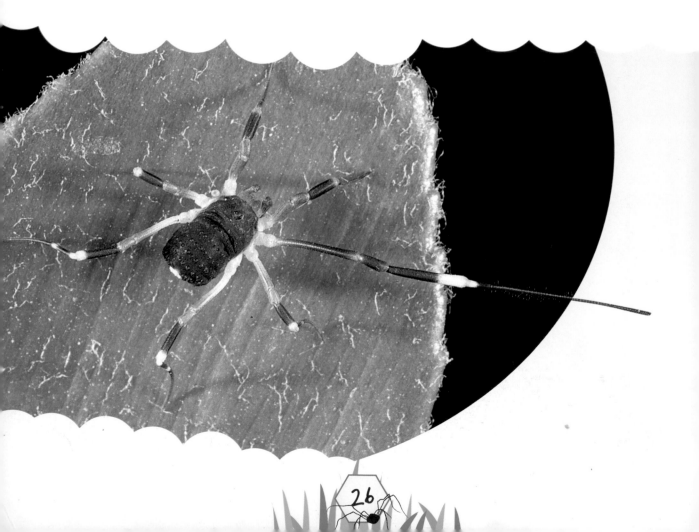

Many daddy longlegs make a smelly liquid to **protect** themselves. The liquid can burn a **predator's** mouth and eyes.

Thinking About Daddy Longlegs

How many body parts does this daddy longlegs have? How many does a real **spider** have?

Why do these daddy longlegs live in a group? Why might it help them to stay safe?

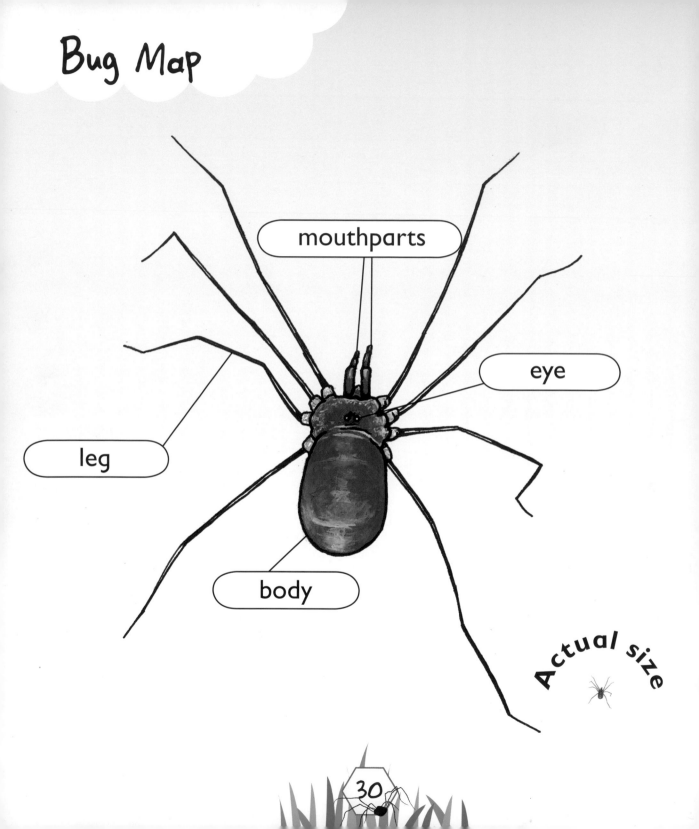

Bug Map

mouthparts

eye

leg

body

Actual size

30

Glossary

arachnids group of animals that includes spiders, ticks, and scorpions

endangered at risk of dying out forever

fang special mouthpart shaped like a claw. It has a tube inside for venom to come out.

habitat place where an animal lives

hatch break out of an egg

female animal that can lay eggs or give birth to live young

male animal that can mate with a female to produce young

mate when a male and female animal come together to produce young

molting time in an insect's life when it gets too big for its skin. The old skin drops off and a new skin is underneath.

parasite animal that lives on another animal and harms it

predator animal that hunts and eats other animals

preen clean. Animals preen their fur, feathers, or skin.

protect keep safe

scavenger animal that finds and eats food that is already dead

spider animal with eight legs that can make silk

venom liquid that can harm an animal

web net made from sticky threads of silk. Spiders use webs to catch food.

Index

arachnids 5

baby daddy longlegs 11, 12

body 4, 7, 9, 28, 30

cellar spider 6

claws 15

eating 16, 17, 18

eggs 10, 11

growing 12, 13

hatching 11

legs 4, 8, 14, 15, 19, 24, 25, 26, 30

life span 22

mating 10, 22

molting 12, 13

mouthparts 17, 30

movement 14, 15, 19

predators 16, 19, 21, 26, 27

scavengers 16

size 8, 9, 11, 13, 30

spiders 5, 6, 7, 18, 28

webs 5, 6

More Books to Read

Claybourne, Anna. *Beetles, Bugs and Pests*. London: Hodder Children's Division, 2003.

Hughes, Monica. *Spiders*. Chicago: Heinemann Library, 2004.

Swanson, Diane. *Bugs Up Close*. Toronto, ON: Kids Can Press, Ltd, 2007.